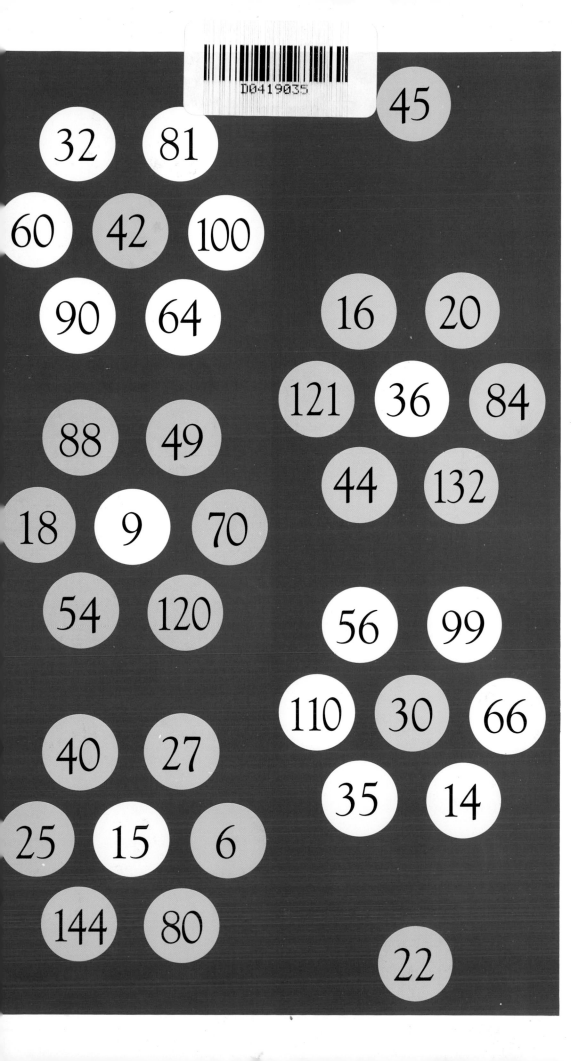

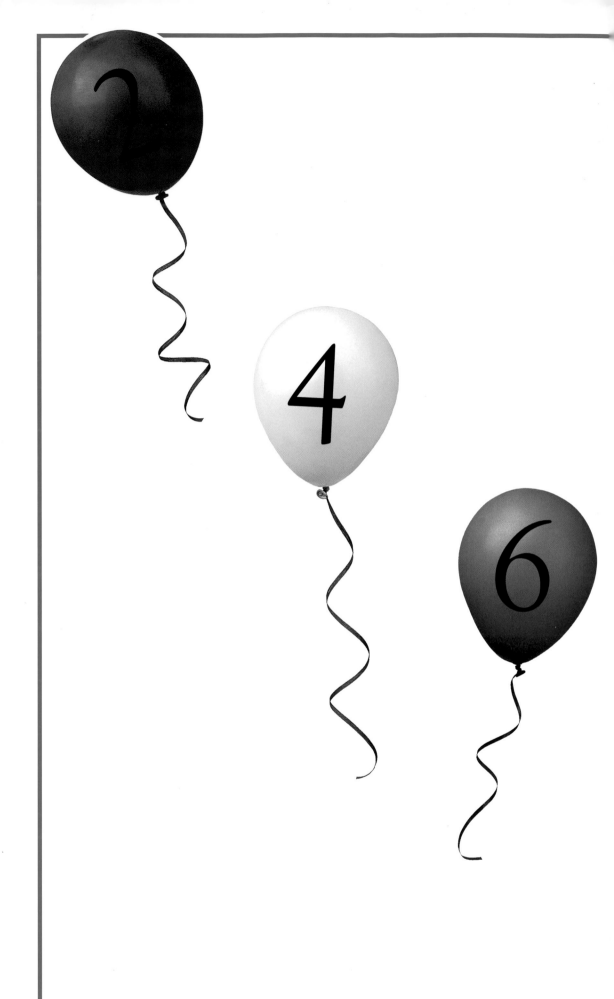

TIMES TABLES!

Wendy Clemson & David Clemson

FAMILY LEARNING

DORLING KINDERSLEY
www.dk.com

from Dorling Kindersley
www.dk.com

The Family Learning mission is to support the concept of the home as a centre of learning and to help families develop independent learning skills to last a lifetime.

Note to parents and teachers

Times Tables! is designed to make the learning and practice of multiplication fun. It presents a variety of number puzzles and novel ideas to allow children to work out multiplication products for themselves. Understanding what happens to numbers when they are multiplied helps children to learn the times tables rather than simply memorizing them. By encouraging your child to try the puzzles in this book, you can help him or her to comprehend multiplication and gain confidence in handling numbers.

How to use the answer decoder

On those pages where the bookmark answer decoder is needed, place it over the panel of numbers so that its coloured edges match the colour bands on the page. The products of the times table will then appear in the windows.

Wendy Clemson and David Clemson

Project Editor Stella Love
Designers Adrienne Hutchinson
and Andrea Needham
Senior Art Editor Jane Horne
Managing Editor Jane Yorke
Managing Art Editor Chris Scollen
Production Fiona Baxter

Published by Family Learning
Dorling Kindersley registered offices:
9 Henrietta Street, Covent Garden, London WC2E 8PS

Copyright © 1996 Dorling Kindersley Limited, London
Text copyright © 1996 Wendy Clemson and David Clemson

10

A CIP catalogue record for this book is available from the British Library

ISBN 0-7513-5377-9

Reproduced by Colourscan, Singapore
Printed and bound in China by Imago

Dorling Kindersley would like to thank the following for their help in producing this book: Photography: Paul Bricknell, Andy Crawford, Philip Dowell, Philip Gatward, Steve Gorton, Marc Henri, Colin Keates, Dave King, Stephen Oliver, Susanna Price, Steve Shott, Jerry Young. Illustration: John Hutchinson and Janos Marffy.

Contents

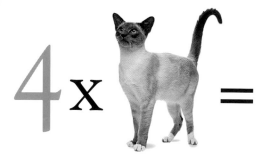

$5 \times$ 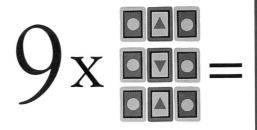 $=$

Five times table 16

$9 \times$ 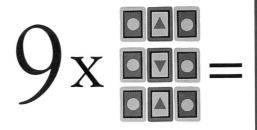 $=$

Nine times table 24

$6 \times$ 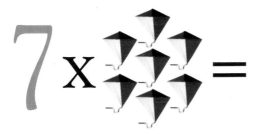 $=$

Six times table 18

$10 \times$ =

Ten times table 26

$7 \times$ =

Seven times table 20

$11 \times$ =

Eleven times table 28
Twelve times table 29

$8 \times$ =

Eight times table 22

$12 \times$ =

Multiplication square 30
Times table wheel 31

All about multiplying

Multiplication is just like counting in number groups.

Can you count the socks in groups of two? Add on two for each pair of socks.

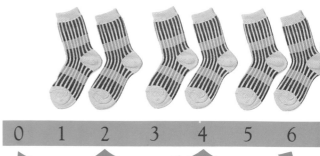

0   1   2   3   4   5   6

Now try to add up these drums in threes.

Can you count the dogs' paws in fours?

Add up the crayons in groups of five.

Each beetle has six legs. Can you count them in sixes?

Here are seven umbrellas. Can you count in sevens?

These dominoes all have eight dots on them.
Can you count the dots in eights?

Can you count up in groups of nine?

Count in groups of ten. See if you can reach one hundred.

How many
balloons will
there be in
two groups
of eleven?

How many
apples will
there be in
three groups
of twelve?

Multiplications

We can write down multiplications, using numbers
and symbols.

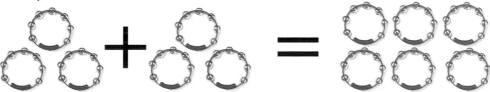

2 groups of 3 tambourines make 6 tambourines altogether.

2 x 3 = 6

This symbol
means groups
of, or multiply by.

This sign
means makes,
or is equal to.

This is
the answer,
or product.

$2x$ Two times table

Lots of sports things come in groups of two.

goalkeeper's gloves   tennis rackets

wheels on a bicycle   running shoes

Count the following in groups of two.

total ?

total ?

total ?

Now try these multiplications.

2 x [bicycle] = ?

7 x [running shoe] = ?

5 x [gloves] = ?

10 x [tennis rackets] = ?

Skate wheel puzzle

There are 2 x 2 wheels on each skate. How many wheels are there in total on a pair of skates?

Can you say the two times table?

$1 \times 2 =$

$2 \times 2 =$

$3 \times 2 =$

$4 \times 2 =$

$5 \times 2 =$

$6 \times 2 =$

$7 \times 2 =$

$8 \times 2 =$

$9 \times 2 =$

$10 \times 2 =$

11

x2

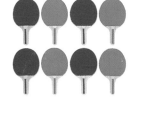
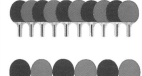

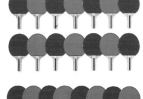
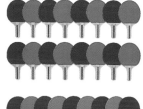
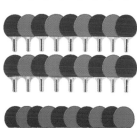
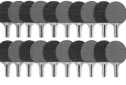

Three times table

A triangle has three sides.

triangle and striker

Count the triangle sides in groups of three.

total
| ? |

total
| ? |

There are lots of other instruments in the music cupboard. Find out how many there are of each one.

drum

tambourine

mouth organ

2 x  = | ? |

8 x  = | ? |

10 x  = | ? |

Guitar puzzle

The guitar has 6 strings. How many strings are there on 2 guitars? How many threes is that?

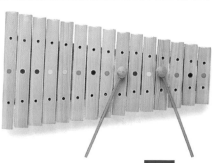

Xylophone puzzle

There are 15 bars on the xylophone. How many threes is that?

Cover up the answers to the three times table. Can you remember what they are?

1 x 3 = 3

2 x 3 = 6

3 x 3 = 9

4 x 3 = 12

5 x 3 = 15

6 x 3 = 18

7 x 3 = 21

8 x 3 = 24

9 x 3 = 27

10 x 3 = 30

Pan pipe puzzle

There are 4 x 3 separate pipes on this instrument. How many pipes is that in total?

Tuneful threes

This group of 3 musical notes is called a triplet.

How many notes are there in 3 triplets?

 Calculator challenge

• The first three answers in this times table are **3**, **6**, and **9**.

• 4 x 3 = 12. Add the digits of the answer. 1 + 2 = ?

• Now add the digits of each answer in the three times table in the same way. What do you notice?

4x Four times table

These animals all have four paws.

beagle   Airedale terrier   snowshoe cat   shorthair cat

Count these paws in fours.

total ?

total ?

total ?

total ?

total ?

total ?

total ?

 Calculator challenge

- Key into a calculator **4 x 4 =** ?

- Clear the screen and key in **44 x 4 =** ?

- Try **444 x 4 =** ? and **4444 x 4 =** ? and so on.
  Is there a pattern in the numbers on the display?

Say the four times table aloud. Check
your answers here with the answer decoder.

x4

1 x 4 =	4	1	5
2 x 4 =	16	8	2
3 x 4 =	12	11	8
4 x 4 =	21	9	16
5 x 4 =	22	20	10
6 x 4 =	12	16	24
7 x 4 =	28	14	30
8 x 4 =	48	32	11
9 x 4 =	36	13	28
10 x 4 =	44	4	40

Pets' corner

6 x = ?   4 x = ?

3 x = ?   10 x = ?

15

5x Five times table

All these craft things come in groups of five.
Use them to help you solve the puzzles.

sheets of paper

stars

paint brushes

modelling clay

crayons

Count in fives to make the total number of things.

total
 ?

total
?

total
?

Multiply to find the product.

4 x  = ?

10 x  = ?

7 x  = ?

1 x  = ?

16

Calculator challenge

- Key in **5 x 5 =** The answer ends in 5.

- Press clear and key in **5 x 5 x 5 =** Does the answer end in 5?

- Multiply 5 by itself lots of times. What does each answer end with?

Pentagons

A flat shape with five sides is called a pentagon.

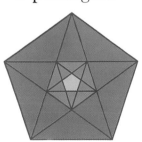

Joining its corners as shown here makes another pentagon inside it. How many pentagon sides can you see?

Can you say the five times table?

1 x 5 =

2 x 5 =

3 x 5 =

4 x 5 =

5 x 5 =

6 x 5 =

7 x 5 =

8 x 5 =

9 x 5 =

10 x 5 =

6x Six times table

All insects have six legs.
Can you count the legs in sixes?

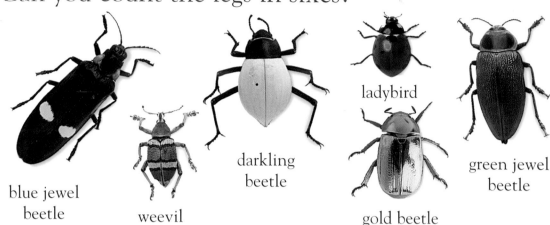

ladybird

blue jewel
beetle

weevil

darkling
beetle

gold beetle

green jewel
beetle

How many legs are in each of these groups of insects?

total
?

total
?

total
?

total
?

 Calculator challenge

- Key into a calculator 1 + 2 + 3 = ?

- Leave in the answer and key in + 1 + 2 + 3 = ?

- Key in + 1 + 2 + 3 = ? again and again.
  What is the pattern of the answers?

18

Work out the answers to the six times table.
Check your answers with the answer decoder.

1 x 6 =	6	17	8
2 x 6 =	11	26	12
3 x 6 =	9	18	20
4 x 6 =	10	64	24
5 x 6 =	30	32	15
6 x 6 =	40	36	30
7 x 6 =	42	37	40
8 x 6 =	90	28	48
9 x 6 =	56	54	63
10 x 6 =	100	63	60

Ladybird puzzle

Every time the ladybird takes a step, all 6 legs move. How many leg moves does it make in 9 steps?

Multiple leg puzzle

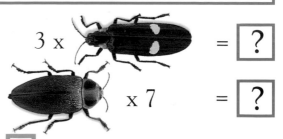

3 x   = ?

x 7   = ?

7x Seven times table

There are seven days in a week.

Sunday	Monday	Tuesday	Wednesday	Thursday	Friday	Saturday
1	2	3	4	5	6	7

Here are four activities that some people do once every day of the week.

have a bath   get dressed   eat lunch   read a book

If you do these things seven times a week, how many times will you do each one during the following weeks?

 x 1 week = ?    x 5 weeks = ?

 x 8 weeks = ?   x 4 weeks = ?

Can you figure out how many days were sunny, windy, rainy, or cold from these weather records?

2 x 7 days = ?   1 x 7 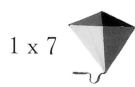 days = ?

4 x 7 days = ?   3 x 7  days = ?

20

Cover up the answers here and check that you know your seven times table.

1 x 7 = 7
2 x 7 = 14
3 x 7 = 21
4 x 7 = 28
5 x 7 = 35
6 x 7 = 42
7 x 7 = 49
8 x 7 = 56
9 x 7 = 63
10 x 7 = 70

 Calculator challenge

- Try keying in **142857 x 1 =** Do you get the answer you expect?

- Now try to estimate the answer to **142857 x 7**.

- Find the answer with your calculator. Do you get the answer you expect this time?

Library book puzzle

This library book is two weeks overdue. If the date is 28th November today, what date should the book have gone back?

Rainbow colours

If there are 7 bands of colour in a rainbow, how many are there in 6 rainbows?

The number eight is used in lots of games.

playing card

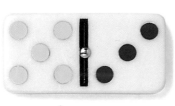
domino

chess pieces

In chess, the two players have eight pawns and eight other chess pieces each. How many chess pieces is that altogether?

chess board

pawns

A chess board has 8 x 8 squares on it. How many squares is that?

Multiply the domino dots and pawns to find the products

5 x [domino] = ?   6 x [pawns] = ?

7 x [domino] = ?   9 x [pawns] = ?

⌨ Calculator challenge ⌨

- Write each answer down as you key in the following:

- Key in **2 x 2 =** ? Then key in **x 2 =** ?

- Keep on multiplying by 2 until you get the answer 64. Which numbers on your list are in the eight times table?

Can you say the eight times table aloud?
Use the answer decoder to check your answers.

x8

1 x 8 =   6   4   8

2 x 8 =   18   16   20

3 x 8 =   23   11   24

4 x 8 =   32   36   22

5 x 8 =   50   40   44

6 x 8 =   48   42   60

7 x 8 =   55   51   56

8 x 8 =   67   64   88

9 x 8 =   77   72   72

10 x 8 =   80   100   88

Card puzzle

There are 4 people playing a card game. The dealer gives each player 8 cards. How many cards are dealt in total?

 Domino dots

In a set of dominoes there are 3 dominoes with 8 dots on each of them. How many dots is that in total?

9x Nine times table

This magician uses the number nine in his tricks.

conjuror's coin

trick card

How many scarves will there be if the magician produces nine of each colour?

mystery cup

magic wand

Try these multiplications.

4 x 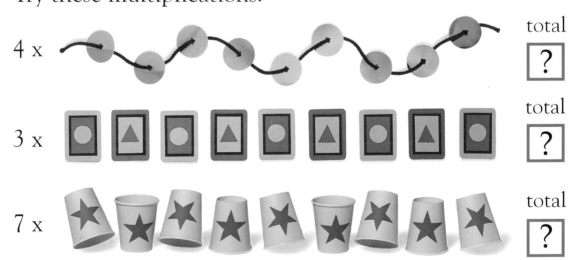 total ?

3 x total ?

7 x total ?

 Calculator challenge

• Key in **121 x 9 =** ? Add up the digits of the answer.
  1 + 0 + 8 + 9 = 18. Then add that answer, **1 + 8 = 9.**

• Now multiply 9 by any number you like. See if you can always add up the digits of the answers to get 9.

Match the answer decoder to the box and check your answers to the nine times table.

1 x 9 =	0	10	9
2 x 9 =	18	20	22
3 x 9 =	9	27	18
4 x 9 =	36	42	37
5 x 9 =	95	40	45
6 x 9 =	45	54	70
7 x 9 =	65	59	63
8 x 9 =	72	71	90
9 x 9 =	18	81	80
10 x 9 =	90	99	89

Magic wands

If, by magic, the 9 wands on this page are multiplied by 2, how many will there be?

Magic one to nine square

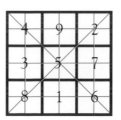

Try adding up any three of these numbers in a row, as marked. What answer do you get each time?

10x Ten times table

Here are some games using the ten times table.

skittles   darts

Score ten points for every skittle knocked over.
Can you work out the following scores?

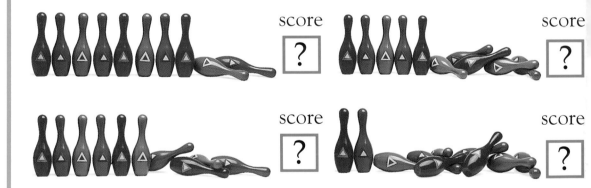

score ?   score ?

score ?   score ?

Multiply the two numbers hit by the darts to find the
scores below. The score of the first go is 3 x 10.

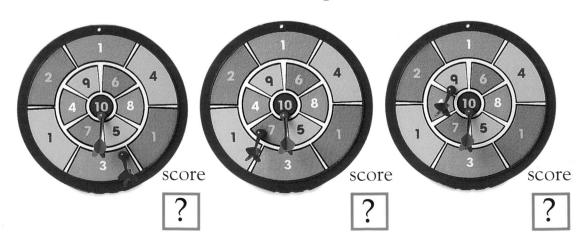

score ?   score ?   score ?

x10

Calculator challenge

- Key in 0.1 x 10 = What answer do you get?

- Press clear and key in 0.1 x 10 x 10 =

- Press clear again and key in 0.1 x 10 x 10 x 10 =

What happens to the decimal point each time?

Hoop-la

If each number is multiplied by 10 to give the score, which pegs must be ringed for the following scores?

? x 10 = 30

? x 10 = 50

1 x 10 =

2 x 10 =

3 x 10 =

4 x 10 =

5 x 10 =

6 x 10 =

7 x 10 =

8 x 10 =

9 x 10 =

10 x 10 =

Eleven times table

Follow the trails to read the eleven times table.

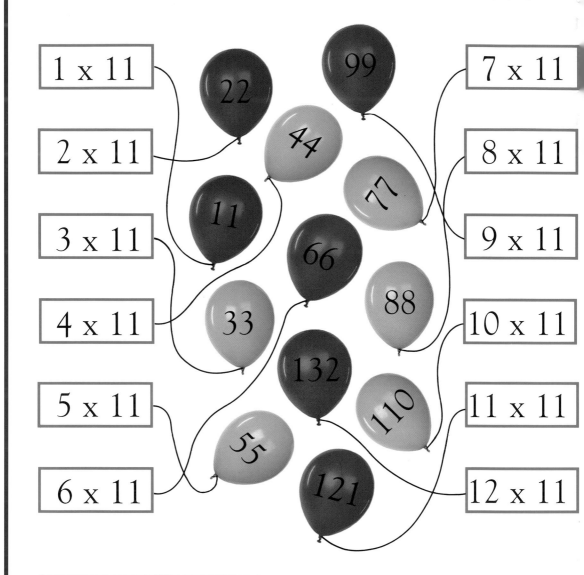

1 x 11

2 x 11

3 x 11

4 x 11

5 x 11

6 x 11

7 x 11

8 x 11

9 x 11

10 x 11

11 x 11

12 x 11

22 99 44 77 11 66 88 33 132 110 55 121

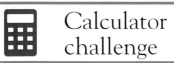

Calculator challenge

- Multiply 11 by itself and try to get this answer pattern.

  1 1
  1 2 1
  1 3 3 1
  1 4 6 4 1

Football puzzle

There are 11 players in a football team. How many in:

3 teams ?

9 teams ?

11 teams ?

Twelve times table $\times 12$

Jump down the steps as you say the twelve times table.

🖩 Calculator challenge 🖩

- Key in **10 x 12 =** ?

- Add that answer to the product of **2 x 12 =** ?

- What other multiples of 12 can you make add up to 144 in the same way?

1 x 12   12
2 x 12   24
3 x 12   36
4 x 12   48
5 x 12   60
6 x 12   72
7 x 12   84
8 x 12   96
9 x 12   108
10 x 12   120
11 x 12   132
12 x 12   144

Apple basket

There are 12 apples in this basket. How many apples will there be in 5 baskets?

Birthday puzzle

There are 12 months in a year. If Tom's 8th birthday is this month, how many months is it until his 12th birthday?

Multiplication square

You can use this multiplication square
to find all the products in the times tables.

This diagram shows you how it works.
Here you can see that **2 x 3 = 6**.

Now look up the products to:

X	1	2	3
1	1	2	3
2	2	4	6
3	3	6	9

$\boxed{6}$ x $\boxed{7}$ = $\boxed{?}$

$\boxed{9}$ x $\boxed{8}$ = $\boxed{?}$

X	1	2	3	4	5	6	7	8	9	10	11	12
1	1	2	3	4	5	6	7	8	9	10	11	12
2	2	4	6	8	10	12	14	16	18	20	22	24
3	3	6	9	12	15	18	21	24	27	30	33	36
4	4	8	12	16	20	24	28	32	36	40	44	48
5	5	10	15	20	25	30	35	40	45	50	55	60
6	6	12	18	24	30	36	42	48	54	60	66	72
7	7	14	21	28	35	42	49	56	63	70	77	84
8	8	16	24	32	40	48	56	64	72	80	88	96
9	9	18	27	36	45	54	63	72	81	90	99	108
10	10	20	30	40	50	60	70	80	90	100	110	120
11	11	22	33	44	55	66	77	88	99	110	121	132
12	12	24	36	48	60	72	84	96	108	120	132	144

Can you see how the halves
of the square on either side
of the diagonal line match?

The red line across
the square is called
the leading diagonal.